CW01513012

Original title:
Zesty Quivers Along the Dragon Pad

Author: Paula Raudsepp
ISBN HARDBACK: 978-1-80559-307-2
ISBN PAPERBACK: 978-1-80559-806-0

Chasing Shadows on the Edge of Feathers

Soft whispers weave through the night,
Delicate wings take their flight.
Glimmers dance on twilight's breath,
Chasing dreams, eluding death.

In the cradle of moonlit sighs,
Secrets linger where silence lies.
Feathers brush against the stars,
Fleeting moments, eternal scars.

Every shadow a story told,
In the chill, the air turns cold.
Echoes linger on the breeze,
Haunting hush of ancient trees.

Whispers of a time unknown,
In the night, we are not alone.
Chasing shadows, finding grace,
In the dark, we find our place.

Wanderlust in the Spine of the World

Mountains rise, a daring call,
Wanderers heed, they feel so small.
Rivers flow like stories past,
In each drop, a memory cast.

Across valleys, through the mist,
Dreams are forged by wanderlust.
With every step, horizons shift,
Nature's touch, the ultimate gift.

Whispered tales of lands unseen,
Adventurers chase where they have been.
In the heart, a fire ignites,
Yearning souls embrace the nights.

Footprints left on sandy shores,
Echoes of forgotten wars.
Wanderlust, a faithful guide,
In the journey, worlds collide.

Enchanted Rhythms Beneath Starry Canopies

Beneath the stars, the silence hums,
In the dark, a heartbeat drums.
Winds entwine with ancient trees,
Whispering secrets through the leaves.

Moonlight dances on a stream,
Carrying forth a silent dream.
Each glimmer a tale to perceive,
In the night, we dare believe.

Songs of crickets fill the air,
Nature's orchestra everywhere.
Rhythms pulse in cosmic grace,
In this realm, we find our place.

Glimpses of worlds beyond the veil,
Lifetimes captured in a tale.
With each breath, the stars align,
Weaving magic, yours and mine.

Fiery Fragments Twilight's Veil

Crimson skies at day's last light,
Fiery hopes take their flight.
In the dusk, the embers glow,
While shadows dance, the night will sow.

Fractured dreams in twilight's grasp,
Each moment, fragile, we hold fast.
Whispers carried by the breeze,
In this stillness, time will freeze.

Stars emerge like scattered gems,
Etching memories of lost diadems.
Through twilight's veil, our wishes soar,
Seeking destinies and something more.

In fiery fragments, hearts entwine,
A tapestry where souls align.
Twilight beckons, a gentle sigh,
As the day bids us goodbye.

Vivid Trails Beckoning the Brave

Paths of gold beneath the sky,
Whispers call the daring high.
Each step forward, fears unwind,
In the heart, adventure finds.

Mountains rise, their peaks so grand,
Footprints left upon the sand.
Nature's beauty, pure delight,
Guides the soul toward the light.

Through the woods where shadows play,
Courage blooms with each new day.
Echoes of the wild abide,
Charging forth, we turn the tide.

Rivers dance with liquid grace,
Every twist, a new embrace.
Brave the storms, let spirits soar,
Onward now, forevermore.

Find the trail that dares the heart,
In the journey, we take part.
With every step, our dreams awake,
Vivid paths, the road we make.

The Unruly Dance of Shifting Winds

Whispers race upon the breeze,
Chaos wraps the bending trees.
Twists and turns in wild array,
Nature's song demands the play.

Clouds collide in tempest's breath,
Lightning draws the line of death.
Yet in turmoil, beauty shines,
Chaos strewn through wild designs.

Winds will shift from calm to fierce,
Hearts may tremble, hopes may pierce.
Spin and swirl like leaves in flight,
Dance with shadows, greet the night.

Breath of freedom fills the air,
With each gust, we shed despair.
Ride the storm where spirits blend,
Embrace the dance that winds extend.

Through the rattle, find your swing,
In the maelstrom, let joy ring.
Life is wild, and we are part,
Feel the winds that stir the heart.

Colors of Wonder in the Heart of Wilderness

Verdant green and sky so blue,
Nature's palette paints anew.
Crimson blooms in sunlit fields,
Joyful echoes, wonder yields.

Golden rays through branches peek,
Nature's voice begins to speak.
A canvas forged from earth and sky,
In the wild, our hopes reach high.

Shimmering lakes reflect the hue,
Frosted edges, morning dew.
In the silence, whispers stir,
Colors deep in dreams occur.

Mountains drape in misty veils,
Adventure flows on gentle trails.
Every view a masterpiece,
In these colors, find your peace.

Wilderness, where wonders call,
In your arms, we lose it all.
Breath of life in every shade,
Grateful hearts in nature laid.

A Secret Map to Forgotten Dreams

Hidden paths and winding bends,
In the silence, truth transcends.
Lost ambitions call us near,
Echoes of the past appear.

Mark the spots where hope was sown,
In the heart, seeds have grown.
Draw the lines with gentle hands,
Mapping dreams across the lands.

Whispers of the age-old quests,
Guide us through life's mighty tests.
Soulful journeys, treasure chased,
In each moment, dreams embraced.

Ink upon our souls so bright,
Charting courses toward the light.
With each step, the past unwinds,
Found in hearts, where fate aligns.

Follow where the compass leads,
In the heart, the spirit feeds.
A secret map between the seams,
Guides us home to frozen dreams.

Wild Whispers in the Moonlit Whisper

In the night, a breeze does sway,
Carrying secrets, old and gray.
Underneath the silver light,
Shadows dance, taking flight.

Whispers soft as leaves that fall,
Echoes from the forest's call.
Stars above, like lanterns hung,
Sing to hearts forever young.

Moonbeams weaving through the trees,
Gently swaying, like the seas.
Nature's voice in hushed embrace,
Finds us all in time and space.

Night unfolds its velvet cloak,
In the silence, dreams evoke.
Every rustle, every sigh,
Binds our souls to the night sky.

And when dawn begins to break,
Golden rays the world awake.
Yet the whispers linger still,
In the heart, they find their thrill.

An Odyssey of Paint on a Whispering Canvas

Colors blend in soft delight,
Brushstrokes dance, a vivid sight.
Whispers of both shade and light,
Craft a story, bold yet slight.

On this canvas dreams are spun,
Each hue whispers 'We are one.'
With a palette rich and vast,
Capturing moments, fleeting past.

Every stroke tells tales of old,
Mysteries in shades of gold.
Brush in hand, heart open wide,
Creating worlds where dreams abide.

The silence speaks in colors bright,
Painting visions, pure delight.
In this realm where voices hum,
An odyssey has just begun.

As layers build, the story grows,
Whispers echo, now it shows.
Art becomes a bridge of fate,
Connecting souls, and hearts elate.

Where Echoes of Delight Reside

In the valley, laughter rings,
Where the heart forever sings.
Every note a sweet reprise,
Echoes dance beneath the skies.

Flowers bloom with colors bright,
Whispers weave through day and night.
Nature's joyful serenade,
In the sun and shade displayed.

Every step on soft green ground,
Brings a melody profound.
Where the breezes gently play,
Life's delight does find its way.

In the stillness, joy takes flight,
Painting dreams in morning light.
Where hope blooms like springtime's flower,
Echoes linger, every hour.

Here in this enchanted space,
Delight resides with gentle grace.
In every heart and every soul,
Echoes call, they make us whole.

Vales of Light Under the Silver Haze

In the vale, soft shadows sway,
Underneath the silver spray.
Light breaks through the morning mist,
Nature's beauty can't be missed.

Whispers twirl like leaves in fall,
Every echo, nature's call.
In this world, where dreams conspire,
Hearts ignite with pure desire.

Sunlight kisses every leaf,
Chasing shadows, banishing grief.
Whispers weave a tale untold,
In the vale, the heart grows bold.

With each ray, the world awakes,
Harmonies that the silence makes.
In this haven cloaked in gold,
Stories of love and life unfold.

Beneath the sky's expansive dome,
In these vales, we find our home.
Where silver hues and light combine,
In quiet beauty, our souls entwine.

The Fable of the Wandering Heart

In the realm where shadows play,
A heart drifted far away,
Searching for a light to find,
Wandering, no peace of mind.

Through valleys deep and mountains high,
The echoes of a distant sigh,
Each step a tale, each turn a song,
The journey felt both right and wrong.

Yet love would guide the restless soul,
With whispered dreams that made them whole,
A fable spun by stars above,
An endless quest, the search for love.

In twilight's glow and dawn's embrace,
The heart would find its rightful place,
No longer lost in shadows cast,
Embracing now, the die is cast.

A wandering heart, now free to soar,
Within the fable, forevermore,
In every tale of joy and pain,
The heart will wander, yet remain.

The Minuet of Spirit and Flame

In the dance of light and shade,
A minuet of dreams is made,
Spirits twirl in graceful arcs,
Their laughter bright, a thousand sparks.

Around the fire, shadows play,
The spirit whispers night to day,
Flames flicker with a tender kiss,
In the warmth, they find their bliss.

Echoes of a long-lost song,
In every breath, where hearts belong,
With every step, a story told,
In the dance, the brave and bold.

As melodies embrace the night,
The spirits soar in sheer delight,
They chase the stars across the sky,
In the minuet, they twirl, they fly.

Through the layers of time and space,
They find the beauty in their grace,
Spirit and flame in sweet romance,
Together forever, they advance.

A Fresco of Spirits Along the Hidden Path

In whispers soft, a story flows,
Upon a path where no one goes,
A fresco bright with hues of soul,
Where spirits dance to make one whole.

Amidst the trees, in shadows deep,
The secrets of the night do keep,
Brush strokes of life, in colors rare,
Each step unveils the hidden prayer.

With every turn, a vision grand,
The spirits guide with gentle hand,
They beckon forth in silent grace,
Along the path, a sacred space.

The air is thick with tales untold,
Of lives once lived, in days of old,
And here within this painted dream,
The spirits join in joy and gleam.

A tapestry of light and shade,
Where history and hope cascades,
A fresco made of hearts and breath,
Along the path, life dances with death.

Intrigues in the Realm of Myth

In the shadows of an ancient tome,
Legends weave, a distant home,
Where dreams and truths begin to blur,
Intrigues whispered, a secret stir.

Gods and mortals play their part,
In the theater of the heart,
With each encounter, tales ignite,
In the realm where day meets night.

Chimeras dance with graceful ease,
Binding souls with whispered pleas,
A puzzle wrapped in timeless lore,
Mysteries open every door.

Destinies entwined, they chase the light,
Along the edge of day and night,
With cunning minds and spirits bold,
In this realm, new stories unfold.

In every glance, a world is spun,
Intrigues blossom, never done,
In the mythic dance, they find their way,
A tale of wonder, night and day.

Luminous Waves on Ancient Pathways

Beneath the moonlit skies we roam,
The ancient paths, now softly known.
With whispers of the night so sweet,
Each step a heartbeat, time's gentle beat.

Waves of silver dance and play,
Guiding us through night and day.
With every breath, the stories call,
Of those who ventured, one and all.

The ocean's breath, a soothing balm,
In rhythmic pulse, it feels so calm.
With every wave, a tale unfolds,
Of ancient times and treasures told.

The stars above, a guiding light,
Through paths of shadows, dark and bright.
We walk together, hand in hand,
On luminous waves, we make our stand.

With hearts aligned, we sail away,
On ancient tides, forever stay.
Our dreams entwined in cosmic flow,
Where night reveals what few do know.

Playful Murmurs Beneath Shimmering Scales

In waters deep where secrets lie,
The playful murmurs sing and sigh.
Beneath the scales that shimmer bright,
A world of wonder, pure delight.

The fish dance freely, a joyful spree,
As currents weave their harmony.
With laughter echoing in the deep,
Their tales of magic, we will keep.

With every ripple, stories spin,
Of brave adventures, where dreams begin.
The ocean's heart, a vibrant play,
In every splash, the world's ballet.

The light breaks gently through the blue,
Creating marvels, always new.
Through shimmering scales, the sunbeams tease,
In playful whispers, the waters please.

Together we dive, lose track of time,
In depths of joy, forever climb.
With each new wave, our spirits rise,
In this waterworld, our hearts devise.

Ecstatic Twirls Through Emerald Shadows

In forests deep, where shadows play,
Ecstatic twirls light up the way.
Among the leaves, where secrets dwell,
A dance of joy, a tale to tell.

Emerald hues form a lush embrace,
As fairies flutter, quicken the pace.
With every turn, the magic glows,
In nature's arms, our spirit grows.

The wind, a partner, guides our flight,
As day turns soft into the night.
Through tangled roots, our laughter rings,
In this vivacious world, our spirit sings.

With every twist, the heart takes wing,
In emerald shadows, we are kings.
The very earth beneath our feet,
Joins in the rhythm, a dance so sweet.

In twilight's grip, we sway and glide,
A whirlwind of dreams, we will not hide.
Through ecstatic twirls, we find our home,
In emerald shadows, forever roam.

Luminous Flutters at the Edge of Night

As day surrenders to night's embrace,
Luminous flutters weave through space.
With wings aglow, they flit and fly,
Dancing shadows against the sky.

Whispers of twilight, soft and light,
Guide the blooms as day turns to night.
In gardens lush where dreams ignite,
The fireflies murmur, pure delight.

With every flicker, the world awakes,
In gentle rhythms, the night partakes.
Stars twinkle bright, a cosmic show,
While luminous flutters dance below.

In secret glades, the magic swells,
As every whisper sweetly tells.
Of journeys taken and loves embraced,
In the twilight's grip, time is replaced.

With hearts aglow, we wander far,
Guided by dreams and a radiant star.
Through luminous flutters, we find our light,
In the tender shadows, at the edge of night.

The Chronicles of Ember and Echo

In shadows deep, the embers glow,
Whispers of tales from long ago.
Echoes of laughter, lost in time,
Guide us through paths, sublime.

A dance of flames, a flickering light,
Stories unfold, igniting the night.
Each spark a dream, each ember a wish,
Held in the heart, like a tender kiss.

Mountains tall, valleys wide,
Adventures await, with fate as our guide.
Through forests thick, we wander far,
Following the trails of our guiding star.

With courage bold, we face the storm,
In the heart of chaos, we find our form.
Together we rise, together we fall,
In the Chronicles of Ember, we answer the call.

As fire fades, new tales will start,
In the quiet glow, we find our heart.
For every echo tells a story anew,
In the chronicles of old, we find what is true.

Splashes of Gold Upon the Canvas of Life

Brush in hand, I paint my dreams,
Colors collide, bursting at the seams.
With splashes of gold, I capture the day,
Each stroke a wish, come what may.

In vibrant hues, my spirit soars,
Life's fleeting moments, I seek to explore.
A canvas unfolds, rich and bright,
In the heart of creation, I find my light.

Each drop of paint, a memory dear,
With laughter and love, I conquer my fear.
In the mess of colors, truth intertwines,
A masterpiece grows, where the heart shines.

Through laughter and tears, I weave my tale,
In the splashes of gold, I shall prevail.
Life's dance of art, forever it flows,
In this beautiful chaos, my spirit glows.

Canvas of dreams, forever I mold,
With every brushstroke, my heart uncovered.
In splashes of gold, my story's alive,
Upon this canvas, my soul will thrive.

Explorations in Spaces Beyond the Known

Stars that flicker, a cosmic dance,
Whispers of worlds, in a timeless trance.
Beyond the veil, where shadows hide,
Explorations call, with arms open wide.

Through galaxies vast, on ships of light,
We sail the skies, in the heart of night.
Each planet's secret, a tale to unfold,
In the depths of space, adventures bold.

Nebulas swirl, in colors untold,
Mysteries linger, waiting to unfold.
In the silence of space, we find our way,
In explorations deep, our spirits sway.

With wonder as our compass, we seek and we roam,
In the vast unknown, we find our home.
Through meteors falling, and comets that sweep,
In spaces beyond, our dreams we keep.

As we journey on, the universe sings,
Of the stories we weave, and the hope that it brings.
In explorations grand, our hearts forever fly,
Through spaces unknown, we touch the sky.

Twilight Journeys Under Fabled Stars

In twilight's glow we softly tread,
The whispers of dreams gently spread.
Fabled stars above gleam bright,
Guiding our hearts through the night.

With every step, a tale unfolds,
Ancient secrets the darkness holds.
Echoes of laughter dance on air,
In mysteries wrapped with tender care.

In dusky hues, our hopes entwine,
Each shadow cast a story divine.
Under the canopy of the night,
Adventure beckons, a sweet delight.

The paths we wander, soft and slow,
Where enchanted rivers gently flow.
Under the watch of the timeless skies,
We find our dreams as daylight dies.

So let us roam, hand in hand,
Through twilight's wonders, a whispered land.
For in this hour, our spirits soar,
Under the stars forevermore.

A Tinge of Spice in Forgotten Glens

In forgotten glens, where shadows play,
A tinge of spice fills the day.
Whispers of nature softly call,
Inviting hearts to wander, enthrall.

The breeze carries scents of old,
Stories of legends that never grow cold.
Among the ferns and the tender moss,
We find a peace, a path to cross.

Sunlight dapples through the leaves,
As time weaves magic, our spirit retrieves.
With every step, a path unspooled,
In this secret realm, our souls are ruled.

Laughter echoes in the rustling trees,
While joyous hearts dance with the breeze.
In the hush of glens, adventure lies,
Waiting to bloom under painted skies.

So hold this moment, rich and rare,
For spice of life lingers in the air.
Embrace the journey where shadows blend,
In forgotten glens, our hearts transcend.

The Harbinger of Whimsy in a Twinkling Grove

In a twinkling grove where wonders lay,
The harbinger of whimsy leads the way.
With every glance, a sparkle shared,
In this enchanted space, we are ensnared.

Fireflies twirl in a moonlit dance,
Inviting us closer, a curious glance.
Colors burst forth, a vivid embrace,
In this symphony of a magical place.

Each leaf a whisper, each branch a song,
In this grove, we find where we belong.
Mysteries weave through the air tonight,
Under the stars, our spirits take flight.

A path adorned with dreams so bright,
Guides us through the loving night.
With laughter echoing, we roam free,
In this twinkling grove, just you and me.

So let your heart, in whimsy, sway,
As the night unfolds, come what may.
For in this grove so rich and rare,
We find a magic beyond compare.

The Caress of Adventure in a Celestial Realm

In a celestial realm where dreams ignite,
The caress of adventure feels just right.
Stars beckon softly, a soothing call,
In this cosmic dance, we give our all.

Galaxies swirl in hues so deep,
Lifting our hearts from slumbering sleep.
Each twinkle a promise, a journey's start,
In the vast unknown, we play our part.

Planets whisper secrets of light,
As we sail through realms, bold and bright.
With every heartbeat, a new path appears,
In this world of wonder, we cast our fears.

Comets trail dreams across the sky,
Painting the night as moments fly by.
Adventure awaits, a beacon so clear,
Guiding us onward, forever near.

So let us soar where the stardust falls,
Embracing the magic that eternally calls.
For in this realm, adventure's embrace,
We find our home in boundless space.

Enigmatic Spirits in Realm's Embrace

In shadows deep, whispers roam,
Where secrets dwell and spirits comb.
A dance of light on the forest floor,
Mysteries linger, forevermore.

Echoes pulse in twilight's glow,
Binding realms that ebb and flow.
Ghostly faces in soft twilight,
Guard the dreams that fade from sight.

Beneath the boughs, silence sings,
Of ancient tales and forgotten wings.
Time stands still in this hallowed space,
Where the past and present interlace.

Eyes of stars in the velvet night,
Guide lost souls to the morning light.
Embrace the magic, the shadows weave,
In this realm, believe and receive.

So linger here, where spirits play,
In the embrace of night and day.
The enigmatic calls, it won't misplace,
Your heart, your soul, in this sacred space.

The Allure of the Untamed Horizon

Beyond the cliffs where oceans roar,
Lies a world untouched, forevermore.
The sky paints dreams in vibrant hues,
Where wild winds sing their ancient blues.

Mountains rise with a challenging face,
Chasing the sun at a fervent pace.
Every peak whispers a daring song,
Inviting hearts that long to belong.

Fields of gold beneath the sun's warm kiss,
Yearn for the wanderer's blissful wish.
Footsteps echo on the untamed ground,
In every contour, adventure is found.

From the valleys low to the skies up high,
Wonders await where the eagles fly.
The allure beckons the spirit to roam,
In every gust, it calls you home.

Embrace the thrill of the open space,
Where nature's hand leaves a bold trace.
With every sunset, dreams intertwine,
On the horizon, life's light does shine.

Glimpses of Euphoria Beneath the Canopy

In a lush embrace where shadows dance,
Nature unfolds its vibrant trance.
Leaves whisper secrets of joy and light,
As hearts awaken to pure delight.

Sunbeams cascade through emerald leaves,
Crafting a tapestry that never deceives.
Colors burst in a radiant display,
Where every glance can sweep you away.

The fragrance of blossoms fills the air,
A symphony crafted with utmost care.
Laughter echoes in a playful breeze,
A moment of bliss beneath the trees.

With every step on the mossy ground,
Foundations of wonder are effortlessly found.
Glimpses of euphoria weave through the night,
Where dreams take flight and spirits unite.

So linger awhile, let the magic show,
Beneath the canopy where love does grow.
In the heart of nature, joy lays its claim,
A glimpse of forever, igniting the flame.

Whims of Fate in Celestial Terrain

In the vastness of the starry sea,
Where fate entwines in destiny's decree.
Every twinkle holds a whispered fate,
Navigating dreams where the seekers wait.

Galaxies swirl in a cosmic dance,
Each journey begins with a fleeting chance.
In the arms of night, possibilities glide,
Whimsy weaves through the celestial tide.

The moon, a beacon in the silent dark,
Guides the wanderer's heart with its spark.
Through nebulous paths, they drift and spin,
In the vast arena where the tales begin.

Stars shimmer softly, secrets to share,
Of love and loss, hope and despair.
Each moment crafted in the loom of time,
Whims of fate—like verses in rhyme.

As comets blaze across night's expanse,
They whisper softly of a fateful chance.
In the celestial terrain, dreams take flight,
While fate dances brightly in the midnight light.

Howling Spirits Through a Mythic Passage

In ancient woods where shadows play,
The howling spirits drift and sway.
They weave through trees, both wise and old,
Whispers of legends yet untold.

Beneath the moon's soft silver glow,
Secrets of time begin to flow.
Echoes of laughter blend with night,
A symphony of ghostly light.

Each step a tale, a haunting song,
They call the curious along.
In misty paths, where few have trod,
Awaits the grace of the unseen god.

With every gust, a story formed,
Through twisted limbs, the spirits warmed.
A dance of shadows, fleeting, free,
Unlocking paths of mystery.

So linger here, in twilight's breath,
Embrace the whispers, dance with death.
For in this realm, the brave will see,
A glimpse of what's meant to be.

A Carnival of Moments in the Emerald Glade

In the emerald glade, where laughter's spun,
A carnival blooms, beneath the sun.
Colors collide in a joyful spree,
Whirling like dreams, so wild and free.

Fresh petals bloom in vibrant array,
Children's laughter brightens the day.
With every heartbeat, the magic grows,
A timeless dance where anything goes.

The carousel spins with a golden glint,
Whispers of wishes in every hint.
Joyful faces, alive with cheer,
Moments are treasures, held oh so dear.

In shadows, the panther softly creeps,
Guarding secrets that the glade keeps.
Yet all is well under the sun's reign,
In laughter and mirth, there's little pain.

As twilight falls, the stars ignite,
Casting spells in the still of night.
A carnival dances, twinkling bright,
In the emerald glade, pure delight.

The Glint of Daring Amongst the Leaves

Amongst the leaves, a glint so bold,
Whispers of secrets, stories unfold.
With daring steps and hearts ablaze,
Adventurers roam through the tangled maze.

The sunlight kisses each emerald leaf,
Inviting dreams, igniting belief.
In shadows cast by the trees above,
Brave souls venture, guided by love.

Rustling secrets in the morning air,
The call of the wild, a daring affair.
With every stride, the path unveils,
Mysteries woven in time's own trails.

A rustle, a flash, a daring glance,
Nature's rhythm invites a chance.
To plunge in deeper, to seek, to find,
The glint of boldness that stirs the mind.

So wander forth, let spirits gleam,
Chase the horizon, follow the dream.
For in the dance of daring leaves,
True magic lives, and the heart believes.

Shimmering Paths to Hidden Dreams

In twilight's glow, paths start to shimmer,
Leading to dreams where hopes grow dimmer.
Yet stars awake with a gentle light,
Guiding the lost through the velvet night.

Emerging whispers from shadows deep,
Carry the wishes that time will keep.
A map of visions in every beam,
Lighting the corners of every dream.

With each footfall upon the trail,
Eclipsed by doubts, but love won't fail.
For hidden dreams await the bold,
In tales of courage waiting to be told.

Take a breath and embrace the unknown,
Let the heart wander, let truth be shown.
For paths of shimmer and light entwined,
Reveal the wonders life has aligned.

So close your eyes, let the journey start,
With shimmering paths that beckon the heart.
Each dream a dawn, each moment a theme,
Together we chase the elusive dream.

Whispered Secrets of the Forest's Heart

Among the trees where shadows play,
Soft whispers call the night to stay.
Moonlight dances on the leaves,
While ancient spirits weave and breathe.

Echoes float on gentle winds,
Carrying tales where magic begins.
The forest hums a timeless tune,
A lullaby beneath the moon.

In hidden glades the flowers gleam,
Where starlit brooks reflect a dream.
Secrets of the earth unfold,
In every nook, a story told.

With soft footfalls on mossy ground,
The pulse of nature, profound.
Each rustling leaf a voice of old,
In silent symphonies untold.

So seek the heart where echoes lie,
In every whisper, a sweet sigh.
For in the forest's gentle embrace,
Hides the world's most sacred place.

Rhapsody of the Wild and Free

Across the plains where wild winds roam,
Nature sings, a vibrant home.
The sun spills gold on fields so wide,
In harmony with joy and pride.

Mountains rise with grace and might,
Their peaks adorned in purest light.
Each valley whispers tales of yore,
Of those who danced and longed for more.

The rivers rush, a joyful song,
In currents deep, where hearts belong.
Wildflowers bloom with colors bright,
Painting dreams in morning light.

From soaring cliffs to ocean's roar,
Every landscape begs for more.
In every corner, life unfolds,
A rhapsody, both fierce and bold.

So lift your voice to skies above,
In tune with earth, in tune with love.
For in this wild, unchained dance,
Life's sweetest melodies enhance.

Daring Journeys Across the Scaled Horizon

Where oceans meet the edgy coast,
The daring sail, the wildest host.
Horizons stretch with every wave,
Adventures call the bold and brave.

With charted maps that guide the way,
Through tempest tides, by night and day.
The sky's embrace, a canvas bright,
As stars unveil their guiding light.

Each journey carved by wind and sun,
A dance of souls, entwined as one.
The stories spun on whispered breeze,
Echo dreams across the seas.

From shores unknown to distant lands,
With open hearts and steady hands.
The thrill of quests that lead us far,
In every challenge, shines a star.

So cast your dreams upon the tide,
Embrace the wild, let fate decide.
For daring journeys, rich and vast,
Reveal the treasures found at last.

Dreamlike Whimsies in Nature's Ballad

In twilight's glow, where visions blend,
The world transforms, as whispers send.
A symphony of hues takes flight,
Where daydreams spark in soft twilight.

With every breeze, a story flutters,
In petals light, and soft woodnutters.
The canvas shifts with every sigh,
As magic fills the velvet sky.

Through glistening dew, the fairies play,
Their laughter brightens up the day.
In every nook, a treasure found,
A harmony that knows no bound.

The rustling leaves, they hum along,
With nature's breath, a lilting song.
In echoes of the wildwood's grace,
Dreamlike whimsies leave their trace.

So wander freely, seek the light,
In every shadow, pure delight.
For in the dance of dusk and dawn,
The heart of nature's grace is drawn.

Secrets of the Sizzling Winds

Whispers flown on summer's breath,
Secrets spun in fields of green.
The sun ignites the dance of death,
In shadows where we've rarely seen.

Ribbons stir with fervent grace,
As twilight drapes the golden sky.
The silence found in nature's place,
Holds tales of what we can't deny.

Softly sighing through the trees,
The winds will carry every thought.
They weave the clues in gentle tease,
Of everything we've ever sought.

With every gust, a story shared,
Of longing, love, and fleeting time.
In essence pure, we linger, dared,
To dance within this sacred rhyme.

Listen close, be still, be wise,
Secrets bared on breezes wide.
In every laugh, the spirit lies,
Together on this wondrous ride.

Glimmers of Frost in the Sunlit Grove

Morning breaks with silver gleam,
Frost-lit leaves in sun's embrace.
Nature wakes from winter's dream,
Soft whispers in a serene space.

Dewdrops glisten, diamonds bright,
Through branches, shadows gently play.
Golden beams weave pure delight,
Inviting warmth to light the day.

Beneath the boughs, a world awakes,
Of stories shared in silent cheer.
Each sigh and rustle gently takes,
The heart and holds it very near.

Colors bloom where none were seen,
Awakening a vibrant throng.
In every brush of subtle green,
The grove sings out its timeless song.

Frost will fade, but memories cling,
In every heart that yearns to roam.
The grove, it sings what spring will bring,
A promise felt, a beckoning home.

A Serenade to the Golden Slumber

As day departs and night unfolds,
A serenade of stars takes flight.
Embracing dreams the heart beholds,
In velvet shades of soft twilight.

Whispers of the moonlit sea,
Hush the world with gentle sighs.
In each note, a mystery,
Where peace and hope forever lies.

Crickets play their evening tune,
While shadows dance beneath the trees.
The silver crescent, a bride of June,
Brings solace wrapped in soothing breeze.

Let go the burdens of the day,
For here, the night sings bittersweet.
With every breath, release, decay,
In golden slumber, feel complete.

Underneath this starry dome,
Our dreams waltz under night's embrace.
In every heart, we find a home,
In every beat, a sacred space.

Breath of the Enchanted Breeze

A waft of air, a soft caress,
Brings tales of lands we seldom roam.
The whispered secrets, light to bless,
With every lift, it speaks of home.

Through shifting leaves, it glides and sways,
Painting each moment with delight.
In golden hues and twilight's rays,
It weaves the day into the night.

It carries fragrance, rich and rare,
From blossoms kissed by morning dew.
A melody of sweet affair,
Of distant dreams and skies so blue.

Within its waltz, the heart takes flight,
As memories trace where we have been.
The smile of time, both soft and bright,
In every breath, the soul's serene.

So let the breeze, enchanted, lead,
With open hearts to cherish all.
In every gust, a loving seed,
A bond of nature's loving call.

Whispers of the Mystic Trail

Through the winding path I roam,
Where secrets whisper, life feels home.
A breeze carries tales long ancient,
In shadows deep, the world is patient.

Soft light filters through the trees,
In silence, I hear the gentle pleas.
Each step echoes the dreams of old,
A tapestry of stories, vivid and bold.

Footfalls dance on earthy ground,
Lost in thoughts, no barriers found.
Nature's voice sings in my ear,
As I tread softly, casting off fear.

With every turn, new wonders appear,
Mystic realms embrace me near.
A journey not just of feet, but of heart,
In this sacred space, I find my part.

The path ahead seems ever wide,
As whispers guide me, by their side.
In the twilight's glow, I feel the grace,
On the mystic trail, I've found my place.

Fragments of Fire and Sky

A spark ignites in the darkened night,
Painting dreams in shades of light.
Fireflies dance in the cooling breeze,
While stars above flicker with ease.

Fragments of glory, fleeting and bright,
With whispers of hope taking flight.
The sky swallows shadows, vast and deep,
In the heart of night, secrets keep.

Each ember holds a story untold,
Of love and courage, both fierce and bold.
As the dawn breaks, colors collide,
Fire and sky now intertwined.

In the canvas stretched above the land,
Passions rise and gently expand.
An aurora of dreams lights the way,
Fragments of fire greet the day.

Through valleys and hills, the colors stream,
Crimson and gold weave the fabric of dream.
In every heartbeat, a promise lies,
In fragments of fire and sky, we rise.

Echoes Through the Emerald Forest

The emerald leaves whisper low,
As ancient woods begin to glow.
Echoes ring through branches high,
Nature's sonnet, a soothing sigh.

In the heart of the forest, time stands still,
Energy flows with a mystic thrill.
Each rustle of leaves tells tales so grand,
Of forgotten lore, whispers of the land.

Through tangled roots and soft moss beds,
Dreams awaken where the river spreads.
Soft shadows dance in the fading light,
Guiding the lost through the enchanting night.

Birdsong filters through the air,
Life's melodious touch everywhere.
In the hush of twilight, I find my way,
In echoes that linger and gently sway.

With every step, I feel it near,
The magic of earth, the pulse I hear.
In the emerald forest, my spirit sings,
Echoes enduring, the joy it brings.

Dancing Shadows on the Lithesome Path

A path unfolds beneath my feet,
Where sunlight and shadows quietly meet.
Dancing figures flicker and weave,
As if the earth wishes to believe.

With every step, the world transforms,
In rhythm with nature, the spirit warms.
Lithesome branches arch and sway,
Inviting dreams to drift and play.

The air is rich with stories told,
Memories woven in threads of gold.
Among the shadows, laughter spins,
In the quiet, new light begins.

Caught in the dance of light and shade,
Time feels fleeting, yet never strayed.
Together we whisper, the path our tune,
As day embraces the rise of the moon.

In this space where echoes dwell,
Magic lingers, weaving its spell.
On this lithesome path, my spirit finds,
Dancing shadows, where the heart unwinds.

The Ripple of Time Beneath the Canopy

In the hush of the forest deep,
Whispers of secrets softly creep.
Sunlight dances on the ground,
Echoes of ages all around.

Leaves sway gently in the breeze,
Carrying tales of ancient trees.
Shadows flicker, memories fade,
Time weaves its intricate braid.

Mossy stones hold the past's breath,
A quiet witness to life and death.
Streams reflect the sky's soft hue,
Nature's canvas, ever new.

Footsteps linger where spirits roam,
In the heart of this verdant home.
Each ripple a story, each sigh a rhyme,
A fleeting glimpse of the ripple of time.

Flames of Passion in the Twilight Mist

In the dusk where shadows meet,
Hearts ablaze with a rhythmic beat.
Fingers entwined, a warm embrace,
In twilight's glow, love finds its place.

Whispers carried on the air,
Promises linger, sweet and rare.
Against the backdrop of fading light,
Two souls igniting the velvet night.

The world melts away, lost in dreams,
Underneath the moon's silver beams.
Flames flicker, passion ignites,
Casting shadows, dancing lights.

Moments fade but love remains,
A fiery spark that never wanes.
In twilight's mist, we softly tread,
Flames of passion, forever fed.

Vibrant Caresses of a Dragon's Breath

In the skies where legends soar,
Fiery breath opens ancient lore.
Wings unfurl, a stunning sight,
Colors blaze against the night.

With each flap, storms arise,
Mysteries linger in the skies.
Vibrant scales shimmer and gleam,
Dancing flames in a bold dream.

Through valleys deep and mountains high,
Echoes of roars that never die.
A guardian fierce, yet warm and kind,
In dragon's breath, magic we find.

Every flicker holds ancient grace,
A timeless dance we all embrace.
In the lore of the evening's hush,
Vibrant caresses, a gentle rush.

Laughter Amongst the Gilded Leaves

Amidst the trees in golden hue,
Laughter dances, bright and true.
Children's voices rise in cheer,
In the autumn's embrace, so dear.

Leaves cascade like nature's song,
Welcoming all, where they belong.
Every crunch beneath their feet,
A melody, a joyful beat.

Sunshine pours through branches bare,
Glints of gold fill the crisp air.
Hand in hand, they skip and play,
In this realm, they find their way.

With every giggle, a moment shared,
In the tapestry of life, well cared.
Together they weave memories bright,
Laughter amongst the gilded light.

Paintbrushes of Light on a Shadowed Passage

In whispers soft, the light appears,
Brushing shadows, quieting fears.
Gentle strokes on the canvas dark,
Illuminate the hidden spark.

Each hue a tale of dreams untold,
Colors blend where times unfold.
In twilight's grasp, the vision shines,
Paths of hope in vibrant lines.

Brushes dance with an artist's grace,
On the canvas of this sacred space.
A symphony of light and gloom,
Painting joy where shadows loom.

With every stroke, a story brought,
In every shade, a lesson taught.
Layers deep, the soul laid bare,
In the passage, light is rare.

So wander through this painted night,
Find your way by inner light.
For in the dark, the colors blaze,
Guiding hearts through shadowed maze.

The Rattle of Laughter in the Dappled Sun

Beneath the trees, laughter rings,
In dappled light, the joy it brings.
Children play with carefree hearts,
In this moment, magic starts.

Giggles echo through the glade,
As shadows dance, no plans are made.
A rattle of joy, a fleeting sound,
In golden hues, their dreams are found.

Sunbeams filter, warm and bright,
Chasing worries out of sight.
Every grin a story spun,
In the embrace of the dappled sun.

Time stands still in laughter's hold,
With every chuckle, secrets told.
A simple world where joy prevails,
In windswept paths and sunny trails.

So let us dance in this warm light,
Embrace the laughter, hold it tight.
For in these moments, life takes flight,
In the rattle of laughter, pure delight.

Mishaps of the Curious Heart

A curious heart seeks to explore,
Through tangled paths and open door.
With every step, a stumble found,
In each mishap, wisdom abound.

With inquisitive eyes, it roams free,
Chasing shadows, wild and carefree.
For every twist and turn leads us,
To lessons learned and hearts that trust.

The road may be riddled with falls,
Yet in each moment, adventure calls.
Through trials faced, we find our grace,
In the curious heart's embrace.

It dances in the face of fear,
Finding beauty in paths unclear.
Through missteps and forgotten dreams,
It learns to flow like winding streams.

So cherish the heart that dares to roam,
For in its journey, it finds a home.
With each mishap, the heart beats true,
In its curious dance, it starts anew.

The Cauldron of Stars in Gaia's Embrace

In Gaia's arms, the stars align,
Their glow a potion, pure and divine.
A cauldron stirs with cosmic light,
Crafting dreams in the velvet night.

Whispers of wind through ancient trees,
Carry secrets on the breeze.
A tapestry woven with starlit threads,
In her embrace, the magic spreads.

The moonbeams drop like silver tears,
Infusing night with hopes and fears.
Within this cauldron, all is bound,
In timeless tales where love is found.

Crystals glimmer, their essence shared,
A dance of fate, the universe cared.
In every pulse, the cosmos spins,
In Gaia's embrace, life begins.

So gaze upon the starlit skies,
Feel the warmth where the earth lies.
In the cauldron of dreams, we ignite,
In Gaia's love, we find our light.

Kaleidoscopic Dreams in Leafy Sanctuaries

In the whispering green,
Colors blend and swirl.
A tapestry of hues,
Nature's soft, sweet pearl.

Sunlight dapples through,
Casting patterns bright.
In each leaf's embrace,
Dreams take flight at night.

Softly rustling winds,
Secrets softly shared.
Every breath a song,
In this realm we dared.

With the morning dew,
Magic fills the air.
A kaleidoscope formed,
In the heart laid bare.

Here in leafy folds,
We lose all our fears.
Kaleidoscopic dreams,
Flowing through the years.

Veils of Mischief in a Dancing Shade

Under branches low,
Whispers start to play.
Shadows shift and sway,
In a mischievous way.

Laughter fills the air,
Echoing around.
In a world of fun,
Adventure knows no bound.

Glimmers in the dark,
Teasing with delight.
Every hidden nook,
Hides secrets from sight.

The moonlight chuckles,
Beneath a leafy grin.
Veils of mirrored joy,
Invite us to begin.

With each twist and turn,
Magic starts to grow.
Dancing in the shade,
Where the wild winds blow.

The Spirited Voyage Across Timeless Waters

Beneath the starlit skies,
A vessel sails with pride.
Wind whispers ancient tales,
As the waves collide.

Each horizon beckons,
Adventures yet unknown.
In this boundless sea,
Our spirits have been grown.

With the sun's warm glow,
We chart our course anew.
Anchored in the dreams,
That we once thought true.

Time drifts like the tide,
Fluid and serene.
Every moment cherished,
In this vast marine.

The journey never ends,
For it's woven tight,
A spirited voyage,
Under the moonlight.

Timid Tides of Adventure's Quest

Along the gentle shore,
Waves caress the sand.
A timid heart awaits,
For the call, so grand.

Crashing tides of fate,
Invite us to explore.
With courage softly found,
We step through the door.

In the salt-kissed breeze,
Whispers draw us near.
Adventure waits beyond,
To quell our every fear.

Each footstep we take,
Marks the path we choose.
Timid tides of hope,
In this life we cruise.

Embracing the unknown,
With a heart so bright,
We dance with the waves,
In the fading light.

Chasing the Celestial Dance

Stars twinkle up high, bright and bold,
Whispers of night, stories told.
Planets align in a cosmic show,
The universe pulses, a vibrant glow.

Galaxies swirl like dreams in flight,
Chasing shadows, embracing the night.
Constellations guide our wandering hearts,
In the dance of the cosmos, magic starts.

Each comet that streaks paints the dark skies,
A fleeting glimpse, a wish that flies.
In the vastness, our spirits blend,
Chasing the cosmic, the journey won't end.

Through the void, we seek and roam,
In the celestial arms, we find our home.
With every twirl, the night sings sweet,
A harmony where our souls meet.

So let us wander where stardust falls,
In the dance of the cosmos, love enthralls.
With hearts wide open, we'll take a chance,
Forever lost in the celestial dance.

Mirthful Murmurs Along the Verdant Way

Among the leaves, laughter weaves,
Nature's song, as the heart believes.
Gentle breezes carry delight,
Whispers of joy in the soft twilight.

The brook babbles secrets untold,
Dancing stones, bright and bold.
Flowers nod in a playful trance,
In this beauty, our spirits prance.

Sun-kissed petals, colors that gleam,
Infuse the air with dreams, it seems.
With every step, the world sings,
Awakening heart to the joy it brings.

Beneath the arching boughs, we play,
In the warmth of a golden day.
Together we roam, hand in hand,
In this paradise, life feels grand.

So let us dance on this verdant way,
Chasing mirth as we laugh and sway.
In nature's embrace, we find our place,
Mirthful murmurs, a sweet embrace.

Essence of Spring Beneath the Stars

Buds bloom brightly after winter's chill,
Nature awakens with vibrant thrill.
Soft whispers of green in the moon's soft light,
Spring dances gently, a serene sight.

Petals unfurl in the fresh morning dew,
Colors burst forth in a grand debut.
Night skies adorned with shimmering grace,
Stars twinkle gently, a timeless embrace.

In the cool air, scents awaken the soul,
The essence of life, a cherished goal.
With each heartbeat, the world comes alive,
In the essence of spring, we thrive.

Crickets serenade the night so sweet,
Nature's rhythm makes our hearts repeat.
Under the stars, we find our way,
In the embrace of a warm spring day.

So let us wander where blossoms bloom,
In the essence of spring, let love consume.
Guided by starlight, we'll find our dreams,
In this magical world, life gleams.

The Lure of the Verdant Vale

A valley lush, with emerald grace,
Whispers of nature in every place.
Mountains rise high, guarding the scene,
In this cradle, tranquility gleans.

Soft murmurs of leaves in gentle sway,
The lure of the vale calls us to play.
Streams sing sweetly, a crystal clear flow,
In the heart of the vale, peace we sow.

Wildflowers dance in the softening breeze,
Embracing the warmth with joyful ease.
In the golden glow of the setting sun,
Together as one, our spirits run.

Beneath the stars, the night unfolds,
A tapestry rich with stories told.
In the verdant vale, dreams come alive,
Nature's embrace helps our spirits thrive.

So come, dear friend, to this sacred space,
In the allure of the vale, our hearts interlace.
With each gentle sigh, under the sky's veil,
Together we'll wander, the lure of the vale.

Crimson Spirals in the Heart of the Forest

Crimson leaves flutter down,
Whispers of autumn's song,
Sunlight dances through the boughs,
Nature's palette, vibrant and strong.

The forest breathes with ancient tales,
Roots entwined with time's embrace,
Echoes of laughter in gentle gales,
A sacred, enchanted space.

Moss carpets the ground so lush,
While shadows play with light,
Softening footsteps in a hush,
In this realm of pure delight.

Crimson spirals twist and twine,
Filling the air with a sense of grace,
Each swirl a story, intertwine,
In this woodland's loving embrace.

Among the trees, dreams take flight,
In the heart of the forest deep,
Beneath the stars that shine so bright,
Awake are secrets we keep.

Electric Breezes Over Jade Canopies

Electric breezes kiss the leaves,
As daybreak paints the sky anew,
Emerald whispers through the eaves,
Nature sings in vibrant hue.

Sunlight dances on the ground,
Golden rays, a warming touch,
In the silence, beauty found,
Every moment means so much.

Branches sway with rhythmic flow,
Nature's pulse a steady beat,
In the breeze, a soft hello,
Life alive beneath my feet.

Jade canopies stretch so wide,
A shelter from the world outside,
Electric sparks of joy collide,
In this sanctuary, I confide.

Each rustle tells a timeless tale,
Of dreams ignited, futures bright,
In this forest, I set sail,
Guided by the morning light.

Sizzling Currents from the Dragon's Heart

Sizzling currents flow like fire,
From the depths of legends old,
Where the dragon's heart inspires,
Mysteries and tales untold.

Embers dance in twilight's glow,
With every flicker, secrets seep,
In the shadows, legends grow,
Whispers from the ancient keep.

Mountains rise to greet the sky,
Veiled in smoke, a timeless myth,
Through the valleys, echoes sigh,
Awakening the spirit's pith.

Sizzling currents, fierce and bold,
Run beneath the starlit night,
Stories of the brave retold,
Guided by the dragon's light.

In the heart, courage ignites,
With every heartbeat, visions surge,
Through the dark, the spirit fights,
In the flames, the dreams emerge.

Spirited Revelations in the Moonlight's Glow

Spirited whispers fill the air,
In moonlight's gentle sway,
Casting shadows, bright and rare,
Guiding lost souls on their way.

Silver beams through branches weave,
A tapestry of night in bloom,
As dreams awaken, hearts believe,
In the magic of the gloom.

Every heartbeat sings a tune,
In the calm of starlit skies,
Underneath the watchful moon,
The universe softly sighs.

Revelations in a dance so light,
As spirits twirl in pure delight,
In the stillness, time takes flight,
Finding peace in the night's embrace.

Awake to wonder, never cease,
In the glow, let shadows fade,
In this moment, find your peace,
In moonlight's embrace, dreams cascade.

Emerald Whispers on Celestial Trails

In the forest's heart, shadows play,
Emerald leaves dance in the sun's ray.
Whispers of dreams float on soft sighs,
Beneath the wide and watchful skies.

Ripples of light, glimmering bright,
Guide the wanderer through enchanting night.
Stars twinkle down like secrets untold,
As paths intertwine, bold and gold.

Moss carpets the earth, a soothing bed,
Where ancient tales of wisdom are spread.
Each step a note in the nature's song,
A journey of echoes, lasting and long.

Time bends and twists in this sacred grove,
In harmony with the pulse of the globe.
Emerald whispers serenade the breeze,
While the moonlight dances among the trees.

Hearts entwined, united as one,
In the whispers of night, the magic's begun.
Celestial trails await those who yearn,
For the secrets of life they long to discern.

Fiery Dances in the Serpent's Embrace

In the jungle's heart, colors ignite,
Fiery blossoms bloom in the night.
Serpents slide through leaves, sleek and bright,
Holding secrets wrapped in their flight.

Flames of passion flicker and twirl,
A dance of shadows, where dreams unfurl.
With every beat, the rhythm calls,
As nature's essence in balance sprawls.

Stars cast their glow on the fiery scene,
In a tapestry woven, wild and keen.
Embracing the earth in a warm embrace,
A hint of danger with every trace.

Echoes of laughter resonate near,
A symphony rising, fierce and clear.
Fiery dances, both wild and free,
Unveil the beauty of life's mystery.

Through the tangled vines, voices soar,
In the serpent's embrace, we crave for more.
A fiery heart in the night does beat,
As nature ignites beneath our feet.

Vibrant Echoes of the Mystic Journey

In twilight's glow, the vibrations hum,
Echoing tales of where we come from.
Mystic paths call with a gentle pull,
Through valleys deep and mountains full.

Colors burst forth, radiant and bright,
Guiding our steps through the velvet night.
Each heartbeat resonates with the earth,
Reminding us all of our shared worth.

Wisdom whispers through the trees,
As the wind carries stories on the breeze.
A journey awaits on this vibrant quest,
Where souls entwine, the brave and blessed.

Stars above twinkle with knowing grace,
As we wander through this sacred space.
Vibrant echoes rise from the past,
Binding us to the world, vast and vast.

Every footstep leaves a trace of light,
A dance of spirits, both bold and bright.
In the depth of night, we find our way,
With vibrant echoes guiding our stay.

Lively Sighs Through Enchanted Glades

Amidst the glades where laughter flows,
Lively sighs drift where magic grows.
Petals shimmer with dew and delight,
As day fades softly into the night.

Whispers of fairies, hidden from sight,
Twirl in the shadows, leaping in flight.
Every sound is a story, sweet and clear,
Calling the heart to draw ever near.

Sunlight dapples with sparkling grace,
Creating a rhythm, nature's embrace.
We dance with the leaves, lose all our cares,
In enchanted glades, where life repairs.

Joy weaves like threads through the air we breathe,
In each lively sigh, mysteries we weave.
Together they sing of the dreams they ignite,
Beneath the soft whispers of the night.

So come take a stroll 'neath the moon's gentle glow,
Through the enchanted glades where the wild things flow.

In every heartbeat, in every song,
Lively sighs remind us where we belong.

Radiant Flights in the Realm of Dreams

In twilight's gentle embrace we soar,
Beneath the stars, we seek to explore.
Wings of light in the silent night,
Floating softly, hearts take flight.

Mirages whisper secrets untold,
Visions shimmer, the dreams unfold.
Each fleeting moment, a treasure found,
In this realm where love knows no bounds.

Through valleys of fantasy, rivers of grace,
Time stands still in this enchanted space.
We chase the echoes, the softest sigh,
As colors dance in the velvet sky.

The moon, a sentinel, guards our way,
Casting spells as night turns to day.
With open hearts, we carry the light,
In wondrous flights, through dreams, we ignite.

Awakening softly, the dawn does call,
Yet dreams linger still, like a tender thrall.
In radiant flights, forever we'll roam,
In the realm of dreams, we find our home.

Thrilling Whirls of the Sylvan Lullaby

In the woods where shadows play,
Whispers weave and leaves sway.
Laughter dances on the breeze,
Nature sings with effortless ease.

Moonlight spills on the forest floor,
Each note a secret, a tale of yore.
Crickets chirp their symphony sweet,
A lullaby that pulls at our feet.

Branches sway in a rhythmic tune,
Underneath the watchful moon.
As night unfolds in a soft embrace,
Time stands still in this sacred space.

The nightingale's song, a gentle guide,
Leads us deeper into the tide.
Rustling leaves, a soothing balm,
In sylvan whirls, we find our calm.

With each passing moment, grace takes flight,
In thrilling whirls, we unite with night.
The forest hums its lullaby sweet,
As dreams take root beneath our feet.

Cobalt Currents of Myth and Magic

Beneath a sapphire sky so deep,
Ancient stories awake from sleep.
Currents flow with whispers of lore,
Myth and magic on every shore.

Waves of cobalt, tales carved in time,
Echoes of heroes in rhythm and rhyme.
From shadows rise creatures of old,
In every tide, their mysteries unfold.

Legends glimmer like stars in the night,
Guiding lost souls with shimmering light.
The sea, a canvas for dreams to paint,
In mythic realms, where spirits faint.

A siren's call, soft yet clear,
Draws us closer to treasures near.
Magic stirs in the ocean's embrace,
Cobalt currents, secrets to trace.

In depths unknown, where wonders reside,
We dive in boldly, with hearts open wide.
For in these tides, the stories gleam,
In cobalt waters, we find our dream.

Serpentine Tempests in the Twilight Mist

Through veils of dusk, the shadows creep,
Whispers of thunder begin to leap.
Serpentine winds weave through the trees,
As twilight's breath stirs the evening breeze.

Lightning fractures the darkened skies,
A fleeting glimpse as the tempest sighs.
Clouds swirl like dancers, wild and free,
In the heart of the storm, we find the key.

The earth shakes softly, a rhythmic pulse,
Nature's heartbeat, an ancient waltz.
Veils of mist hide secrets untold,
In tempests fierce, we dare to be bold.

Electric dreams collide and clash,
In the storm's embrace, our spirits thrash.
Yet still we find a beauty bright,
In serpentine tempests, a dance of light.

As dawn approaches, the clouds unwind,
Leaving behind whispers of the blind.
In twilight's aftermath, we stand reborn,
From tempests woven, a new day is born.

The Luminescent Play of Dice with Destiny

In shadows cast by fate's own hand,
The dice are rolled upon the sand.
Each turn unveils a path anew,
Where fortune smiles, or bids adieu.

With careful breath, the game unfolds,
In whispers soft, the future molds.
What chance may bring, we dare to seek,
In leaps of faith, we find the weak.

Through trials faced, the heart's delight,
In laughter's glow, through darkest night.
The dice may clatter, and secrets flee,
Yet, in the game, we're wild and free.

Each roll a tale, a thread of fate,
In luminescent dreams, we wait.
With every score, a song to sing,
In destiny's dance, we feel the swing.

As lights aglow, the world spins bright,
And shadows fade with morning light.
To trust the journey, bold and wise,
In life's grand play, we win the prize.

Threads of Adventure in Tapestry's Fold

In fabric woven, tales combined,
Each thread a quest, a world defined.
Through valleys green and mountains high,
Adventure calls, it will not lie.

With footsteps firm on cobbled street,
We chase the sun, where strangers meet.
A whisper here, a glance exchanged,
In heart's embrace, lives are arranged.

The loom of fate spins colors bold,
In patterns rich, the stories told.
With wonderlust, we grasp the loom,
To stitch our dreams, dispel the gloom.

Each journey starts with vibrant thread,
In tapestry's fold, our hearts are led.
The edges fray, yet still we mend,
In crafted dreams, our spirits blend.

Embrace the journey, wild and free,
In every strand, our legacy.
For in the weave, new paths arise,
In threads of adventure, we find the skies.

The Soft Embrace of Twilight Fantasia

In twilight's glow, the day departs,
A soft embrace around our hearts.
With stars like whispers in the night,
The world awakens, pure delight.

In shadows deep, the dreams take flight,
In vibrant colors, slipping light.
The moon's caress, a tender kiss,
In moment's grace, we find our bliss.

As fireflies dance and laughter sways,
We lose ourselves in evening's haze.
A symphony of night engages,
In every breath, the magic stages.

With hands entwined, we stroll the line,
Of dreams and hopes where spirits shine.
In every whisper, tender, true,
The soft embrace creates anew.

When night enfolds, the past may fade,
Yet in this moment, love's displayed.
In twilight's arms, forever stands,
A world reborn through gentle hands.

Twilight's Euphoria in the Dragon's Lair

In hidden realms where shadows dwell,
A dragon stirs and weaves a spell.
With eyes like embers, fierce and bright,
It guards the dreams of endless night.

In twilight's arms, the whispers rise,
A tapestry of muted skies.
With every beat, the heart ignites,
In euphoria, the soul invites.

With scales of gold and wings that soar,
The dragon roars, a thunderous score.
In realms of magic, treasures gleam,
Each breath a story, each roar a dream.

In the lair's depths, the shadows play,
Where ancient tales anew display.
In twilight's glow, we seek our place,
In dragon's heart, we find our grace.

As night unfolds with secrets shared,
In every glance, we're unprepared.
For in this space, where legends breathe,
Twilight's euphoria, we believe.